THE FALLEN FEATHERS

Nadakkavu, Kozhikode, Kerala, 673011
www.insightpublica.com
e-mail: insightpublica@gmail.com
Title: **The Fallen Feathers**
(A Collection of English Poems)
Author: **Phalgunan Thekkethalakkal**
First Edition: October 2022
Cover Design&Layout: kjvj@insight

Printed and Published by
InsightinPublica Printers & Publishers Pvt. Ltd.
ISBN 978-93-5517-218-1

THE FALLEN FEATHERS

(A Collection of English Poems)

PHALGUNAN THEKKETHALAKKAL

INSIGHT PUBLICA®

Phalgunan Thekkethalakkal is a retired English teacher having teaching experience spanning more than 29 years in various educational institutions.

He had also served as a district resource person in English for more than 16 years. He was one of the authors of 'Mukulam' resource handbook published by Kannur district Panchayath. He was also included in the on-site support team to promote quality-based education in the district. He had completed his graduation in English from Payyanur college and attended St.Thomas College, Thrissur to obtain his M A degree. He also completed another postgraduate degree in English from Madurai Kamaraj university. He earned his B.Ed degree from RIMSE, Mysore. Phalgunan started his career as a teacher in Bharath Vidya Bhavan private college, Payyanur. Later Worked in AVSGHSS Karivellur, and Mathil Ghss. He was also a Plus- two teacher and Former Vice- Principal of PES Vidyalaya, Payyanur. He is now living in Karivellur, Kannur Dt.Kerala. The author can be accessed at: karivellurphalgunan@gmail.com

POEMS

THE GOLDEN SHOWER TREE 9

RETIREMENT 11

A PRAYER 13

IN THE FIELDS AGAIN 15

KALEIDOSCOPE 16

CHILDREN IN THE RAIN 18

BOUQUET 20

FLOWERS FORGOTTEN 21

THE UNINVITED GUEST 23

THE RAIN ON THE WAY 25

A GROUP PHOTO TAKEN 27

THE RIVER OF YESTERYEARS 29

MY SCHOOL ON A SUNDAY EVE 32

BRAVE SONS, OUR MIGHTY WARRIORS 34
WAITING FLOWER SELLER 35
THE VISITOR 36
THE LION AND THE HUNTER 37
THE SONG OF THE LANDLESS 39
ON TEACHING 41
THE ECLIPSE 43
BEING ABNORMAL 45
THE DEITY OF KARIVELLUR 46
MONSOON 48
THE MOTHER WHO LIVED AMONG US 50
WHEN FATHER LIVES 51
HOME SWEET HOME 52
THE DRAMA OF LIFE 54
THE GYPSY GIRL 55
ON RETURNING AGAIN TO THE OLD WAYS. 57
BUDDHA, THE REDEEMER 59
COILED MEMORIES 61
THE FALLEN LEAVES 63
LESSONS 65
DEVI MOOKAMBIKA 67
CLOSING WINDOWS 69
THE BOATMAN 71

THE GOLDEN SHOWER TREE

I brought a sapling
of Indian laburnum and
hoped it would grow like
a decoration during festivals.
The sapling like a child
needs attention on the land
where I planted, near
the corner of my home.
It refused with leaf one,
and never shown a sign of life
as it was there etched forever.
My dreams withered and fell,
and the golden flowers I imagined
in its glory during Vishu[1] days.
I watered it, cared for it well
like a baby and it didn't smile,
no tender leaves sprouted to pity me.
I visioned it would die soon,
a plant desires patience and silence.

---

1 Vishu: A festival celebrated in Kerala during the month of April.

One leaf in it, it struggled,
life was so hard, stem dried
for a long length of two months
remained there, didn't stoop,
silent and steady in the battle
of being forgotten forever.
Oh! Today I have seen it great,
bears fresh green leaves like tears,
aging with the strength it upholds
murmuring a lesson like a spell:
lead we are all with hopes unsaddled
in our ways of tears and sorrows.

RETIREMENT

To retire from a job is not an easy business,
that makes a rare respite and lull, to leave
a bundle of care and anxieties rolled upon,
the morose, melancholy attire of routine
that you were wearing in harnessing life.
Looking for stops, your free will reigns,
your mind that wound and coiled in
duties released like pollen from dry seeds,
and duty is undone can't be shaken off
for it claims your way of earning bread.

.

You are set free as a free bird at will,
opened out from the cage of care,
fluttering and fillip forward for sure,
with unsteady wings as you know,
the aim still clouded in a mist of gloom.

.

The pent-up thoughts poured in,
after you are alone in the vast sky,
for you earned the job by unyielding race,
made first in the heat and hard work,
winning efforts plenty in the tournament.

That was your sustenance and life,
reaching your aged behaviour,
ruled it in time for a timely release,
an order of pension and sanctioned;
earning a farewell in deep tears,
find your walk in a forgotten way.

●

A PRAYER

Oh! God save us from
the maladies thick and black,
coil around the world
like a serpent to bring an end.
So simple my prayer be,
free us all like as before,
as flying kites shall ever be.
Feel jealous of the birds,
now the same with all animals,
even about ants and antelopes.
Is it Your wish and judgement
that we move around with masks,
like an ornament in suffocation?
Grand us the life-giving air,
all the time Your blessing,
we know is endless, everlasting.
Oh! God miserable are we,
so sorrowful and imprisoned,
in the pitch darkness, a pall of gloom:
as marriages and funerals attended
a few in fear, feel the same.
Oh! God save us from the darkness,

when the world creeps in through blind ways,
and unseen foes filled the sky.
Merciful as Your name suggests,
lift us, elevate us, breathing
a new life on us at Your will.
We pray to You, have no others except You
to seek a shelter and refuge, bless us,
with a hope unredeemed, a light
and brightness that ever shines
through the heart of the world.
●

IN THE FIELDS AGAIN

Long I desire to be alone,
in the rice fields where,
I meet to rebuild my past
memories of childhood days.
Those days were gone,
in thc ricc ficlds near the canals,
wading through the pristine
waters with the shining fish.
Now in these days of the pandemic,
I went there once again;
is it a mistake or a way forgotten,
I was through the ridges in the shower,
amidst the gazing rice reeds.
Alone, alone I walked in rain,
at a distance, no one was found,
only a farmer at a glance I viewed,
and I was with a mask on my face,
like a soldier armed to beat the scourge.
Is it a blessing to be in nature,
getting those easy gales and green,
I could have breathed the air so fresh,
but lo! I forgot to untie my mask.

KALEIDOSCOPE

God has a kaleidoscope[1]
that frequently He frets,
at his will, once in a century
to make the world upside down.
Diverse shades reflect,
colors of life formed
in an optical symmetry,
displace its forms,
some lives turn up,
and others fall down.
The designs and desires,
the scope He shakes,
the poor comes up,
while the rich comes down,
'The large numbers', He says,
'enjoyed their joyous dance,
hence they are in their graves,
then those submerged in sorrow,

---

1 A Kaleidoscope is a toy consisting of a tube containing three long slides of mirrors tied in a triangle shape and if we put pieces of coloured paper, changing patterns are visible.

be lifted up, let their lives thrive'.
Oh! God save the world,
save us from your experiments,
for we are helpless without You,
shower your mercy on our souls.

●

('As flies to wanton boys, are we to the gods, they kill us for their sport'--
William Shakespeare)

CHILDREN IN THE RAIN

Rain gives me a tongue,
for utterance frequented,
like splashes, waters and,
the little drops trickle on the face.
The long-dead memories,
sprout leaves at this moment,
crowded, when rain furious,
fall its living presence.
Back in life, we were children then,
school going and the torrent of rain,
conspiring in the months,
of monsoon in June and July.
The rotten, deserted,
muddy waters embrace our way,
I ran back to those memories,
running and laughing with the rain,
the smell of new books, dresses,
and the umbrella, so enticing.
Oh! I have to leave those,
visions as nobody wants them;
those desires and angels,

in tune with the new ways of life
when rain is nothing but,
a routine, a weather forecast.

●

BOUQUET

I thought of making
a bouquet of life,
it occurred to me that,
there it strewed the past
and present of my hopes
and a vine so green
entwined with the future.
A bouquet of my dreams,
vivid aspirations,
laced many flowers,
and I was proud,
of being an owner of one.
But fate's pastime,
decreed otherwise;
it broke and shattered
my bouquet conspired
to throw it to an endless
chasm of loneliness.

●

FLOWERS FORGOTTEN

Flowers are many
in this world;
but who cares about these
smiling faces
in the shrubs, in the forest.
People call them wild,
as they were wild born,
but often men pass by,
mutilate them by crushing,
footsteps are so sad.
I closely look at the tiny,
cute, beautiful flowers,
violet, pink, red, and blue,
like studs worn by girls.
Why should I forget them,
since they watch us closely,
separated and lonely
with their blowing charms.
I remember them with pain,
that I collected them as a child,
festivals bring an occasion

to make floral designs.
Man is born for forgetting,
he chases beauty anew,
flowers he made and bought,
Dhalia, Rose and Chrysanthemum.
The petals I saw were natural,
bloom to teach a simple life,
spread its radiance unseen,
show us what is truly beautiful.

●

THE UNINVITED GUEST

He is everywhere,
the uninvited guest.
Nobody knows from where
he comes and goes.
But in your world, he is
like a shadow accompanying:
since he knows your pauses
and frantic gestures in life.
He doesn't come invited,
so enigmatic and mysterious,
follows you till he decides
to take your memories forever.
Has ever an Emperor,
or a king challenged him?
Alexander died so was
Timur and Napoleon.
Countless men and women,
perished in the cycle of life,
the imminent hour of death.
Can he be called a friend?
Beggar or a king, rich men

and the poor, all came in line,
and beautiful celebrities,
vanished wearing a pall of gloom.
Why do then these struggles,
war on territories and religions?
Politics blindfolded, groping in,
all go behind the curtain once.
Unaware of his icy cold hands,
place on your shoulder;
but you don't feel that
your veins pulsate not forever.

THE RAIN ON THE WAY

Bathing in the rain,
I forsake the world a bit,
unsung sorrows, miseries that nurse
all plights hollowed my cheeks a lot.
Clouds, darkness, song, and rhythm
of the rain long and less cared,
drive me to the land of
the long-drained memories.
Time flies since it with wings
carries us all the way
to the clouds of forgetfulness.
We like puppets, obeying orders,
feeling the live drops dribbling,
on my face, clothes drenching,
I think what it was to be,
during the distant childish days.
I like to spend the day indoors,
under the watchful eyes of burdened duties,
that make the wheels of routine,
sitting lazy, alone watching the splashing rain.
Umbrella I carried, felt the rain out,

an urgency to move out,
the rain welcomed, embraced me,
a long pent-up emotion, oh! my cold friend.
Such love, it showers on me?
I remember the rain when I was a boy
going to school drenched, protecting books,
with plastic sheets covered.
Don't we need to be closer to him?
An old friend for the time being forgotten
made us happy as we were children of nature.
Now we scarce think of going out in the rain.
I forget all my worries about rain,
Amen! I do like to be free,
my mind in fathomless solace,
in the mist, walking in the rain.
Meet and greet the rain on the way I say,
nothing bothers your mind to bleed,
neither politics nor pranks or any question
on you being either left or right.

●

A GROUP PHOTO TAKEN

It was a group photo of your will,
where you can't miss any gaps to fill,
just on the right line to your friend,
while the left was on to a trend.
All came, you and your foe[1] it assumed
that he came to be a mince you presumed,
but on the light glimmering,
your hate long despondent came to a halting.
'Smile', he said behind a technical face,
to a boy who chewed a melancholy lace,
that nobody except him a line to be mended,
that line, badly gone and a boy there be sent.
'Line by line ladies first and men next,'
broken in diseased sunlight[2],
expecting an absorbing glare;
all eyes conspired a focused stare.
You sit there and brave a tact,
that told you to change the pose and place,
needs another pose just below a girl,

1 Foe: A friend with whom you are displeased.

2 Diseased sunlight: evening.

who trickles on your alarm of fitful glance.
You weathered to look so foolish,
upon a face where the camera rested to halt,
'Two times took' he said and the flash was gone,
and 'the final 'there made an absolute turn.

●

THE RIVER OF YESTERYEARS

Oft I wonder I see the river[1],
meanders of an unknown way,
as she doesn't know her real way,
to be mistaken as a wanderer
who doesn't know his way.

She likes to go where
the trees in a row stealthily cover,
to hide the treasures of oblivion,
far removed of sorrowful like,
gets people the stories of myth.

The coconut trees are like an arch,
protects, she bounces a leap,
where she has not been blocked,
and knows the ethics of humanity,
the agonized men of the shore.

---

1 River in Payyanur assumes different names in different villages.

The way she goes finds a bridge,
the road and the column witnesses
all cars, motors, men and women,
during the past untamed and challenging.

The pillars work not as an arch,
but it gets people remembered
the lapse of life, on both sides,
the guards of time ever remained.

In monsoon, she is red hot brown,
the rivers of force find not her inferior,
Where she gulps all the mud to prolong the motion,
during unwanted stayed away aloof.

She bears different names,
as a boy called by his mother of love.
the names varied from one village to the next,
and one name is sweet as the other in the text.

She is much sung by the erudite,
from her inspiration to form lyrics,
of a reputation of the farthest skill,
earned fame all over, still of flourished milk.

In my time of college days,
oft I peeped at her with awe,
that from buses she gave a quick view,
of treasure and stories left unknown.

She had seen me grow, all the boys,
out of their academics, to their fame,
for they went and returned to be greeted,
and high they flew and saw her majestic pillars.

The entrance of the town,
where ancestry coupled with the struggle,

and there it gave all the sinews
in support of freedom and its tremor.[1]

All watched the shore bracelet lined,
there, the money-spinning machines,
so rude a machine to support,
to get laid with timbers that wrought.

Does she despair any hands
in search of her treasure of wealth?
The fish and oysters are uncountable,
and the boatman knows her well,
to move with a song every time with hope.

So she flows miles counting miles,
in her origin called another name,
in the fields and to the boys it's known,
and again to inspire them with a form of love
far emptied, as the river of yesteryears.

●

1 Freedom and its tremor: freedom movement.

MY SCHOOL ON A SUNDAY EVE

Silent memories touched, lone
I reached the school I studied,
on a Sunday eve in careless hours,
she embraced me, a son in her arms.
Loneliness entered and vibrated,
those past reveries of distant yore,
I smelt all thoughts sprouting
and the emptiness sits like a hound.
The benches I sat on, the board I peered
to calculate the painful figures,
and I saw the teacher with his cane,
the tears, fear, and laugh intertwined.
There aroused the faces so angelic,
my classmates in a dream or a vision,
who looked at me with their joyful pranks,
melted in the red rays of the dying sun.
The shadows deepened, the beams,
the arches, the playground, and shouts,
all painfully gone in the cycle of time,
never to be reborn again, with the passage of life.
I bade a farewell to the silent hours,

filled in darkness, a pall of gloom,
that hall of fame and frames,
etched in my heart, marked forever.

●

BRAVE SONS, OUR MIGHTY WARRIORS

Warriors of our nation,
mighty and matchless,
brave sons so fearless,
pierced the enemy garrison.
They command all and,
no force makes them less.
They roared and crushed,
scattered were the dead.
They charged like wind,
Their arms shined,
blinded the faceless cowards,
stooped them to sleep forever.

●

WAITING FLOWER SELLER

On the wayside, he sits,
since the morning he has waited in vain,
with each small bagful,
of flowers left unsold.
The man waits and no one cares,
or he is not a big seller of flowers,
nothing to sell except his dreams,
his face turns dim with the evening sun.
Among the shouting and cries,
he sits silent like a milestone.
I feel like a bit of advice given to him,
'wail and cry stand up and shout'.
No soul came, for people are rich,
in the order, he is a poor seller of the poor.
looking at each person passing by,
his frame fumes and heaves hope.
In the evening sunlight of desire,
he found standing like a statue,
a residue, a froth or a scum,
of the stream of life cast ashore.

●

THE VISITOR

Eyes widened, she spotted the spider,
it stops on a wall, there a while,
rest in intention, half awake,
'Look', she said, 'danger works in an eight-legs spread,'
'it is a mission, I said in awe,
addressed a fear that sinks her mind to a bloody low,
'it pays a visit quiet; long intended,
cherishes its wish at home, contended.'
It reaches its legs a little more,
in spasms, calculated to reach a wall,
broods a little as it climbs above all,
like an evil design, its legs designed,
'Poisonous', quipped she, with a broom,
lashes she along the wall it rests,
so proud of the tiny jumps on the table,
on the books, so curious creeps to find its way.
All along the house in the morn,
it was a prowl for the creature alone,
turning its touch on the wall, on the shelf,
it emits its life at risk all alone.

●

THE LION AND THE HUNTER

The man entered the forest,
he is a hunter of Lions,
an expert as he used to be,
killed a number of Lions,
as he knows the way with Lions.

He knows how to kill it,
as hunting Lion is
a life-death game.
You miss a wink of care,
and court death for sure.
The hunter knows as advised,
his father was a good hunter.
The lesson he practiced,
and recollected in hunting
that the king of the forest,
his tail he circles three times
before its jump, and the gun
aims and fires its head
before its jump.

The lion roared and the hunter
made his spree aiming the gun
to shoot it before the third.
But the lion didn't circle its tail,
and he jumped killing the hunter
saying," I too had a father
who advised me not to,
circle tail before a hunter."

●

THE SONG OF THE LANDLESS

We exist in loneliness,
thrown away into the bin of negligence,
brutally a mind forced to burn,
that defeats sadness and pain.

Homeless are we nor a name,
we live in the shaded corners,
of the city enlarged and kept in,
the solitary side of the pavement,
hearing your footsteps that
tear our hearts and souls forever.

You won't find anything human in us?
There is no separation
between our tribes since all of us
make one name, and all over
trumpeted as tramps and beggars.

The ugly shade we live in,
covered with torn clothes and rags
as a membrane of shame,

deep-rooted in us to force
our eyes laden with tears,
go with the drops of rain
and dried with the heat of summer.

we are born with nature, weathered
to learn her pulse like
animated dolls, dance in tune
with her beats and drums.

The sun goes down as planned
when neon eyes open yellowish,
shadows painted us melancholic,
and night creeps in, darkness reigns,
under the stars pulsating like shining beads.

we are nothing but froth or scum,
a residue dusted at your will,
silent and marginalized,
find our broken sleep and
dreams when numbness creeps in.

●

ON TEACHING

Teaching is not a bothering
to those who might be
dipped in themselves into the
heavenly ocean of wisdom.

But for others who
struggle hard for words
of utterance, it is like telling a story
unprepared and half cooked.

And you teach lessons,
better make it digested,
coating with cream of humour;
after all, you aren't a dictator.

Advice you give all
to clear their ways
since their steps would be altered,
fallen and faltered to difficult ways.

Show them the lights,
as a torch bearer and
you must always think
in terms of virtues embodied.

●

THE ECLIPSE

We don't need to search
for darkness, an eclipse.
It is here and there when
men and women dwell,
forgetting themselves.

It is here with lies,
uttered with a thousand tongues,
It is here with those words
preach hate and treacheries
over caste, politics, religion, and race.

It is here when a wail of sorrow,
makes us deaf and dumb,
being to turn us helpless and frozen
since no hand lifts us,
from the dungeon of devils.

Darkness is everywhere,
when justice is a false word
playing in the hands of the rich,
It remains stagnant,

when the poor are suppressed,
and the tears of women,
flow like rivulets.
Life as ever be,
we live with a hope
as we know an eclipse is not eternal.

●

BEING ABNORMAL

You are safe when
you neglect a person
in a critical stage.
But otherwise, you are abnormal,
as justified by a friend,
'Why should you take the trouble?'
The gulf returnee
felt his burden he unloose,
he missed an opportunity
to cheat his employer.
'You are abnormal, You fool,
Why can't you betray him and amass millions?"
You react against injustice.
But nobody was there to bell the cat.
you jump into the fray and lost.
People turned to be deaf and dumb,
That is normal and always be.
Be honest, don't tell lies,
and not a liar I want to be.
I tell the truth and troubles in scores courted,
And the voice says,' You abnormal,
Why can't you tell a simple lie to escape?

●

THE DEITY OF KARIVELLUR

Mother! you are an ocean of love
far beyond measures and your eyes
so divine; look and pacify our hearts,
and the deep wounds of life's miseries.
Upon the long stream solitary we row,
life provides jungles of thorns,
You are the guide and hope and light,
in the deep shadows of anxieties bound.
The holy form you wear, the flowers,
decorated, soothes my heart of pain,
the kindness showers on us, Oh! virgin
and the blessing you give is everlasting.
The goddess of Muchilot as we pray
knows no barriers, as every one Her children.
The temple she resides in is an abode,
a shelter of never-ending peace.
There are legends and lore infinite,
that remember Your virtue and wisdom,
indomitable that make You omniscient.
defeated the gentry proud and arrogant.
expelled, You, oh! mother came to the village,
the event is written as a supreme sacrifice,

that made the goddess as we see Her today,
of the great incarnation for the poor.
The festival celebrates marriage,
of the goddess where people like a flood,
come where they receive Her blessing,
and provided with sumptuous food.
The kaliyattam[1], not for the old and young,
But for the children, they enjoy it a lot.
They are the semblance of Her, happy and playful,
and be seen as the images of the Mother.

●

1 Kaliyattam: the grand theyyam festival in North Malabar.

MONSOON

She arrives with a few drops
of kisses gently on my face;
the dewy melodies of monsoon
herald new hopes in the fields.
I hear the sounds of distant rain,
like an army charging,
killing the drought-stricken
land of thirsty roots, a cold blessing.
Nothing sprouted in her absence,
she delayed all with awe;
with withered leaves, empty bowels of the earth,
hear the trumpeting dance of rain.
Blowing wind and dancing trees,
jhankaar beats[1] and lightening,
sounds so familiar and it vibrates
all, a new life never explained.
Children splash the streams,
waters, spoiled in rivulets that,
gush forth in their ways of wanderings,
with paper boats of desire and dreams.

---

1 jhankaar beats : A popular Hindi musical;Thundering.

How can I forget these showers,
deepened my soul with a sense of touch,
the humanity that spreads and pervades,
all with beetles and dancing blades of grass?
She forgets herself in blessing,
with days of songs spanning weeks,
and all we remember are the cloudy sky,
waters, puddles, and swelling rivers.

●

THE MOTHER WHO LIVED AMONG US

Teresa oh! mother your name divine,
not for living life alone;
for you made a life not yours,
but for others who lived in tears.
You die an angel, the ocean of love,
spasms into the heart of orphans
who are broken in the wheel of life,
thrown away int to the old bin of negligence.
You lived among them as one among them,
a mother to touch their sins as your own,
to you, their worst pestilence didn't scare,
with a merciful look and endless care.
The saint of Kolkata, born incarnate,
to allay the tears of the alleys,
the world bowed before thee the sacrifice,
to a light immortal, an everlasting flame.

●

WHEN FATHER LIVES

When father lives, you are a sprite,
a son so young and careless of
your wayward ways, thinking nothing
that bothers you to the bottomless pit.
You don't care as you may not feel,
anything grave and the whole world
rings with you and the world belong to you.
No feeling makes you down so soft and serious.
He cares for you since nobody cares,
like the sun his glory is endless.
He has limits but played his game so well,
within his boundary line, and bade you farewell.
When father dies, something breaks away
yourself and your semblance with you
that accompanies you always all the time,
and you feel like your shadow removed.
Life is a stream, seems endless,
as poets' say', You have to row and row.'
Now you feel you are a man so grave,
and your face tells it so well to travel alone.
sprite-a small creature in stories, using magic and playing tricks.

HOME SWEET HOME

Home sweet home,
after a long back home,
where you spend the hours,
with solace, and endless comforts..
It invites us where ever we are,
when we move life like a trolley
hard to earn our existence,
soothes our hearts however small may be.
We falter all the way alone,
the valley of hellish designs,
like in a forest we explore,
miseries, sorrows, and painful deeds.
Back home like a mother,
she wants to heal your wounds,
of sadness and ills,
take your spirits elevated.
Again, home is a place,
where you get love, brings relief,
and it's the place where the mother resides,
father resides, wife and children.
Home is also one's beloved country,

motherland whom we offer our blood,
a way of sacrifice, all we can do,
for the memories, home sweet home.

●

THE DRAMA OF LIFE

There were times when
we were children,
ever readied to play folklore,
a funny sequence of life's shore.
characters beasts and men,
occupied our hearts then,
innocence braided like beads,
of a chain, wore always on the ways.
Now chasms[1] made us forget,
as each one dragged to target,
joys, those fruits in a dark terrain,
of life's drama inviting pain.

●

---

1 Chasms: the passage of time

THE GYPSY GIRL

The way which winds to the woods,
no matter how it came there to be,
as chance would have a wayfarer
that I came there in touch with grace.
I leaped to the twigs and touched them,
and it said 'no' to me and came again,
that bent to bless me there again,
or tried to tell secrets unknown to me.
the marsh over there gleamed,
and like gold, it turned and beamed,
eyed and glorified by the rays,
of that distant red round wonder.
the trees that laced to be,
on each branch, it wore a jewel,
of that dim rays of the sun,
presented, and each step to care.
curious it was, there my eyes,
that chanced to see some rays
that delved deep to the valley yonder,
where shepherds whistled their joyful care.
Dim as it was the evening,
threw the light as it dwelt

on every crevice, rock, and stone,
laid over me a shadow so melancholic.
sound as it was, that betrayed my ear,
an owl in that dim daylight, in a voice so foul,
warned my forward steps,
like a long story foretold.
There emerged a girl of woods,
I bore an air that surpassed
the degree of fear not crouched,
On that sad -borne evening,
nor I looked at her with hope.
Did I look over her as she was,
just like a vision of mischief?
No animal or bird I saw
but something sent like a fox.
'Stop', your next step over there, She said
'is to die to the abyss nearer,
where your bones are to be kept
forever in an ever-lasting crypt.'
The girl said the words and seen no more,
vanished among the leaves and gone,
Nobody knows from where she came,
a child of elf, mist or fog, I knew not,
but the words did save my life.
●

ON RETURNING AGAIN TO THE OLD WAYS.

Driven from the routine,
When spasmodic life,
turns me like a top,
it was like a message sent.
soon I found myself there,
in the festival ground the' kaliyattam'
so eventful vibrates the village,
all enthralled and enlivened.
All my manly arrogance and nature
I wear, like a shell I found myself
inside where pride reigns in,
scarcely met I with people's eyes.
Men and women in standing arranged,
devote their mind to god and goddesses,
who came before their praying eyes
with oracles consoled their woes.
I moved a little and stood to watch' theyyams'
The cosmic dance in tune with drums,
raised Their hands to shower

blessings, predicting a wise world.
The air of pride dulled my senses,
soon vanishing, stopping at the sanctum,
like a child, I felt and saw the promising deities,
and I turned everywhere and walked around.
I was busy from one place to another,
searching shops and windows selling water
colored, near the vendor selling cheap sweets,
gathering a spring of youth long past gone.
I remember, I remember, when I was a boy,
I liked moving too, hearing the tunes,
of whistles and blowpipes, balloons and drums,
sensing the sweetness of a thousand ice sticks.

●

BUDDHA, THE REDEEMER

Towering abode of God,
the arch of the pagoda invites,
the tired traveller who
steps into a stately shrine of peace.
The prayers count on,
the mind doused in the holy shrine,
the monks sing in praise,
the mighty forsaken sage.
Mind and body mired in mud
and filth, swim in worldly sins,
oh! lord elevate us, You prince,
left Your kingdom for our sake.
The gongs, beats, and beads[1]
chanting prayers delving deep,
into our souls, oh! raise us,
light our ways to thee forever.
Your silent, deep meditating,
omniscient, silent face
showers a soothing rain,

---

1 beads --rosary,

on our deserted, bare minds.
Oh! You the enlightened spirit,
Bodhisattva[1], the incarnate,
give us a glance as you care,
all to leave off the shores of pain.

●

1 Bodhisattva-the incarnation of Buddha through ages before Gautama Buddha. The poem was written on the occasion of my visit to the Tibetan monastery, Coorg, Karnataka.

COILED MEMORIES

"Beware of snakes in the waters,"
warned the old man who weaves
hopes and yarns of life in a shed.
"Stupid to play there you scoundrels,"
wading the waters to school,
I waited for her, my friend,
I remember she was my neighbour,
one year older waited for me often.
the waters splashed, turned transparent,
logged, there was torrential rain,
the fish small glistened its shape,
leaped like herons evade in the eve.
We waited and collected some flakes[1],
held our kerchiefs on both sides,
and lo! we saw a snake, a water snake,
not poisonous, but others are not.
The day I waited for her in the morn,
but she came not, my companion,

---

1 flakes-small fish
This poem is a tribute to my childhood friend who died prematurely.

I asked the men going to her home,
and they gave me the most ominous glance.
I ran to her home, and cared not about men,
who talked in discussion "snake"
in the yard, I saw her last, covered in white,
a smile radiating, and eyes filled with dreams.

●

THE FALLEN LEAVES

The years that have gone by,
never-never come back,
like fallen leaves,
they bring decayed memories.

Often I think I would go,
to visit my place where
I studied, the schools, colleges,
but nobody knows me there.

Where are my friends,
oh! where are they?
Who walked with me,
cracking many jokes,
and being funny, strong
in their arms to lift,
anything that life offers.

Silently we separated,
being alone walked slowly,
and others departed,
to a world of oblivion,

carried by the wings of death.

We moved in our ways,
and walked memories haunted,
appears like a vision
vibrating afresh, so aromatic.

There your lonely walk in the
blind, long alleys of the maddening world
that treat you with many shapes
sorrows, joys, and ugly turns.

Why do you bother them?
They bade you goodbye,
and went to higher places;
we often step on these fallen leaves,
with its nerves never regained.

LESSONS

The boy didn't answer
the question on vowels.
I repeated, "Didn't you get
time to read or study?"

He didn't write
an appreciation
of the poem I dissected
many a time.

and never brought his
own version of the opinion,
he can't write well,
wasting his time.

He bowed his head,
admitted mistakes,
I slowly knew about him,
that he sells newspapers.

His father is no more,
and mother struggling,
with diseases that even
doctors lost count of.

He didn't know,
what is a simile,
metaphor or rhyme, and
he can't take pleasure,
out of a poem,
or sees beauty in a rose
or new showers.

Is it a big crime?
Nor is it a crime
that you don't watch
movies every week
when a hundred men
miss their lives in the storm.
There are lessons still to learn.
●

DEVI MOOKAMBIKA

Mookambika is Durga incarnate,
the power of Saraswathi and Lakshmi,
the mother killed the demon Mooka,
hence hailed as Mookambika.

the most sorrowful souls
find solace in You, give them,
Thy blessings like the new showers,
and save the deserted souls.

You are my hope, my refuge,
when the fire of fate throws me
to the never-ending dungeon
of the burning miseries of life.

Bear with me, lift my heart,
from the flesh, and torment
of evil-headed desires,
as Mother, She knows.

Mother, as everyone prays,
with a divine smile wipes their tears,
the light removes the darkness,
brings wisdom to deranged minds.

●

CLOSING WINDOWS

Closing windows,
a man sits indoors,
making life his shell,
he is the resident evil.

the world he makes his own,
doesn't bother the roars,
of pain, injustice, and miseries,
for he doesn't look through once.

With his long legs, he steps,
for his own selfish needs,
his family is all he likes,
like a cocoon he ruminates.

The man like a snail,
sits in his office, prunes
the accounts he derives,
longing benefits he shares.

sitting around the corner,
he digs WhatsApp, Facebook
munches dirty news,
back again like a roosting bird.

●

THE BOATMAN

The swift flow of the river,
is given to me on this cold night,
a long jettisoned and marooned life;
To row the boat in the dark along,
that frets the body it belongs.

I do this journey of sinews,
and I look at the moon that recedes,
away up in the clouds that sail,
like a forlorn ship over its puffed sails.

I stop this ride as the toil of hours ended,
today is long pent up and etched,
on the sidelines of the efforts dried,
with the sweat of my nerves and arms,
sleep tames my charging dogs of desire.

In my dream, I see a thousand boats,
all are hopes, beautiful sails frankly attired,
I trip like a drunkard who set his steps,
not to fall in the pageants of life.

●